SOUTH AMERICA

Alexis Roumanis

www.av2books.com

AV² provides enriched content that supplements and complements this book. Weigl's AV² books strive to create inspired learning and engage young minds in a total learning experience.

Your AV² Media Enhanced books come alive with...

Audio
Listen to sections of the book read aloud.

Video
Watch informative video clips.

Embedded Weblinks
Gain additional information for research.

Try This!
Complete activities and hands-on experiments.

Key Words
Study vocabulary, and complete a matching word activity.

Quizzes
Test your knowledge.

Slide Show
View images and captions, and prepare a presentation.

... and much, much more!

LET'S READ
AV² BY WEIGL™
ADDED VALUE • AUDIO VISUAL

Go to **www.av2books.com**, and enter this book's unique code.

BOOK CODE

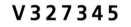

V327345

AV² by Weigl brings you media enhanced books that support active learning.

Published by AV² by Weigl
350 5th Avenue, 59th Floor New York, NY 10118
Websites: www.av2books.com   www.weigl.com

Library of Congress Cataloging-in-Publication Data

Roumanis, Alexis.
  South America / Alexis Roumanis.
     pages cm. -- (Exploring continents)
Includes bibliographical references and index.
ISBN 978-1-4896-3046-9 (hard cover : alk. paper) -- ISBN 978-1-4896-3047-6 (soft cover : alk. paper) --
ISBN 978-1-4896-3048-3 (single user ebook) -- ISBN 978-1-4896-3049-0 (multi-user ebook)
1. South America--Juvenile literature. I. Title.
F2208.5.R68 2014
980--dc23

                              2014044134

Printed in the United States of America in Brainerd, Minnesota
1 2 3 4 5 6 7 8 9 0 18 17 16 15 14

122014
WEP051214   Project Coordinator: Jared Siemens
                              Design: Mandy Christiansen

Weigl acknowledges iStock and Getty Images as the primary image suppliers for this title.

SOUTH AMERICA

Contents

3

Welcome to South America. It is the fourth largest continent.

This is the shape of South America. North America lies north of South America. Antarctica sits to the south.

Where Is South America?

Arctic Ocean

Arctic Ocean

North America

Europe

Asia

Pacific Ocean

Atlantic Ocean

Africa

Pacific Ocean

SOUTH AMERICA

Indian Ocean

N
W   E
S

Antarctica

Two oceans touch the coast of South America.

South America is made up of many different landforms. Deserts, mountains, plains, and rainforests can all be found in South America.

The Patagonian Desert is the largest desert in South America.

Lake Maracaibo is the largest lake in South America.

The Amazon Rainforest is the largest rainforest in the world.

Mount Aconcagua is the tallest mountain in South America.

The Amazon River is the longest river in South America.

9

The three-toed sloth moves more slowly than any other mammal.

Jaguars are the largest cats in South America.

The tapir is the largest land animal in South America.

South America is home to some of the world's most unique animals. Many different kinds of animals live there.

The giant tortoises of the Galápagos Islands can live more than 100 years.

The green anaconda can grow to be 30 feet (9 meters) long.

South America is home to many different types of plants.

The potato plant comes from the Andes Mountains.

The tomato plant was first grown in South America.

The pineapple plant was first found in South America.

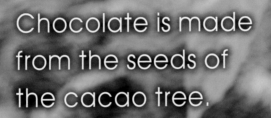

Chocolate is made
from the seeds of
the cacao tree.

South America grows
much of the world's
coffee beans.

Venezuela is one of the oldest countries in South America. It is more than 200 years old. People have lived in South America for thousands of years.

The Inca are one of the first peoples of South America.

Many kinds of people live in South America. Each group of people is special in its own way.

Inca wear bright colors to the Festival of the Sun.

People wear masks at Carnival in Brazil.

People in Peru wear large hats made of wool.

Gaucho is a style of clothes worn by farmers in Argentina.

17

More than 410 million people live in South America. The country with the most land in South America is Brazil.

The city with the most people in South America is São Paulo, Brazil.

There are many things that can be found only in South America. People come from all over the world to visit this continent.

Angel Falls in Venezuela is the highest waterfall in the world.

Machu Picchu in Peru is more than 500 years old.

Los Glaciares National Park in Argentina has the largest ice field outside Antarctica.

The statue of Christ the Redeemer in Rio de Janeiro is 98 feet (30 m) tall.

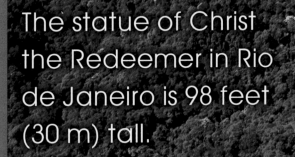

The Nazca Lines in Peru are best seen from an airplane.

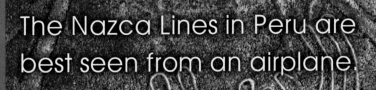

South America Quiz

See what you have learned about the continent of South America.

What do these pictures tell you about South America?

KEY WORDS

Research has shown that as much as 65 percent of all written material published in English is made up of 300 words. These 300 words cannot be taught using pictures or learned by sounding them out. They must be recognized by sight. This book contains 70 common sight words to help young readers improve their reading fluency and comprehension. This book also teaches young readers several important content words, such as proper nouns. These words are paired with pictures to aid in learning and improve understanding.

Page	Sight Words First Appearance
4	is, it, the, to
7	of, this, two
8	all, and, be, can, different, found, in, made, many, mountains, up, world
9	river
10	animal, any, are, land, more, moves, other, than, three
11	feet, grow, home, kinds, live, long, most, some, there, years
12	comes, first, from, plants, was
13	much, tree
15	for, have, old, one, people
16	at, each, group, its, own, way
17	a, by, large
19	city, country, with
20	only, over, that, things
21	an, has, lines

Page	Content Words First Appearance
4	continent, South America
7	Antarctica, coast, North America, oceans, shape
8	deserts, lake, landforms, plains, rainforests
10	cats, jaguar, mammal, sloth, tapir
11	anaconda, Galápagos Islands, meters, tortoises
12	pineapple, potato, tomato
13	chocolate, coffee beans, seeds
15	Inca, Venezuela
16	Brazil, colors, festival, masks, style, Sun
17	clothes, farmers, hats, Peru, wool
19	São Paulo
20	waterfall
21	airplane, ice field, Rio de Janeiro, statue